HARRISON

ENCYCLOPEDIA
of PRESIDENTS

William Henry Harrison

Ninth President of the United States

By Christine Maloney Fitz-Gerald

Consultant: Charles Abele, Ph.D.
Social Studies Instructor
Chicago Public School System

 CHILDRENS PRESS ®

CHICAGO

William Henry Harrison,
ninth president of
the United States

Library of Congress Cataloging-in-Publication Data

Fitz-Gerald, Christine Maloney.
   William Henry Harrison / Christine Maloney Fitz-Gerald.
      p.   cm. — (Encyclopedia of presidents)
   Includes index.
   ISBN 0-516-01392-0
   1. Harrison, William Henry, 1773-1841 — Juvenile
literature.   2.   Presidents — United States — Biography —
Juvenile literature.   I.   Title.   II.   Series.
E392.F57   1987   87-16842
973.5'8'0924 — dc19   CIP
[B]   AC

Picture Acknowledgments

The Bettmann Archive — 83, 88

Historical Pictures Service — 9, 12, 13, 14, 17,
20, 21, 22, 25 (top), 29 (2 pictures), 32, 33, 40,
43, 49, 50, 53, 54, 56, 59 (2 pictures), 60, 63, 65
(2 pictures), 68, 69, 70, 71, 74, 79, 84, 87, 89

Courtesy Library of Congress — 4, 5, 6, 18, 44,
72, 76, 80, 85, 86

Nawrocki Stock Photo — 15

North Wind Picture Archives — 8, 25 (2 bottom
pictures), 31, 52, 57

Photri — 67 (top)

H. Armstrong Roberts — 34, 67 (bottom)

U.S. Bureau of Printing and Engraving — 2

Cover design and illustration by
Steven Gaston Dobson

Childrens Press®, Chicago
Copyright ©1987 by Regensteiner Publishing Enterprises, Inc.
All rights reserved. Published simultaneously in Canada.
Printed in the United States of America.
   ? 3 4 5 6 7 8 9 10 R 96 95 94 93 92 91 90 89

A handkerchief produced for Harrison's 1840 presidential campaign

Table of Contents

The birthplace of William Henry Harrison in southern Virginia

Chapter 1

The Northwest Territory

The road was wide enough. Other than that, a worse road for wagon travel would be hard to find. It was rocky, rutted, and unpaved, with more than its share of both steep inclines and low boggy spots. The soldiers felt sure they were working at least as hard as the mules that pulled the wagons. When the wagon wheels sank in mud, stuck in ruts, or stopped on hills, the men pushed and pulled the wagons forward with sheer strength.

The scenery was pleasant, though. The wooded hills of Pennsylvania shone a rich red and gold in the October light. Among the soldiers was eighteen-year-old ensign William Henry Harrison. He and eighty other new soldiers had left Philadelphia almost three weeks earlier. They were now approaching Fort Pitt, which would later be known as the city of Pittsburgh.

The U.S. Army was small in 1791 — not even five thousand men. Although the revolutionary war was over, a soldier's life was still dangerous. Many soldiers lived in log stockades in the Northwest Territory, where the Indians were fighting the white settlers. Life on the frontier could be brutal and short.

Traders often offered liquor to Indians in trade for animal skins.

The Northwest Territory of the 1790s stretched from the Appalachian mountains in the east to the Mississippi River in the west. Its southern border was the Ohio River. Its northern border was Canada. The Indian tribes living there were strong. Before the revolutionary war, the British had not allowed settlers there, because they wished to protect the fur trade. After the Revolution, the land suddenly opened up to white settlers. People poured over the mountains and found a beautiful country. There were forests of giant trees interspersed with open grassy meadows. The southern areas were hilly, with the land becoming flat and swampy in the north, around the Great Lakes. To the west, the prairies began.

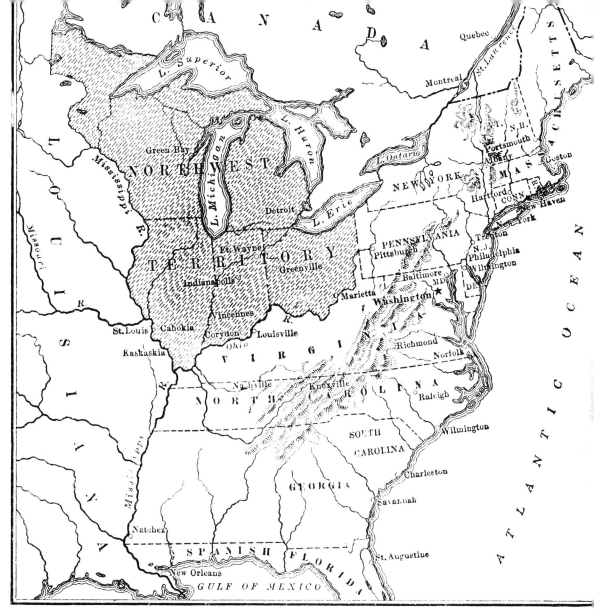

Map of the Northwest Territory, showing the states later created from it

The Northwest Territory would someday become the states of Ohio, Indiana, Illinois, Michigan, and Wisconsin. In the 1790s, it was held by Indian tribes who would not give up their ancient homelands without a fight. Many young American men joined the army at this time to take part in that fight.

Army life was so difficult that most men who joined were desperate. Some were running from debts. Some were running from the law. Others were so poor that they joined for the meager pay—eight dollars to sign up and three dollars a month thereafter. Then there were those who joined for adventure. William Henry Harrison was one of these.

He didn't look much like a soldier. Tall and lean, with a long, thin nose, Harrison looked like the scholar that he was. Mile after mile he trudged along with a book by the Roman writer Cicero in his backpack. The new ensign was the son of a famous father. Colonel Ben Harrison was one of the original signers of the Declaration of Independence, back in the dark days when American independence from Great Britain looked far from certain. William Henry was the youngest of the colonel's seven children. He was born on February 9, 1773, in the family's brick mansion, Berkeley. Berkeley stood by the James River in southern Virginia.

As a child, William Henry was taught at home by tutors because there were no schools nearby. When the revolutionary war was going badly for the Americans, Colonel Ben moved his family to a different house. It was a wise move. Soon after the family had left, enemy troops paid a call on Berkeley. The soldiers dragged every stick of furniture and every shred of clothing from the house and burned them in a huge bonfire. All of the cows and horses were stolen or shot.

When he was fourteen, William Henry was able to enter Hampden-Sydney College. He wasn't there long. His father became annoyed with the school's religious teaching and pulled his son out. Next William Henry was apprenticed to a doctor in Richmond. But the colonel was soon unhappy again. His son had taken up with a "bad" crowd—abolitionists. Abolitionists wished to see all of the slaves freed—and the Harrison wealth was based on land and slaves. Colonel Ben was fuming. It wasn't long before William Henry found himself enrolled in medical school, this time in Philadelphia. A short time after he arrived in the city, his father died. William Henry inherited some land, but Berkeley and most of the family money went to the eldest son, Benjamin. Benjamin did not continue to pay for his brother's schooling.

So William Henry turned his back on the study of medicine and joined the army. His officer's commission came from President George Washington himself. After signing up, William Henry visited the man his father had named as his guardian, Robert Morris.

Morris was an old friend of Colonel Ben Harrison and a talented financier. This Philadelphia patriot had put all of his skill to work to find money to help the Revolutionary Army. Morris was shocked to hear that his old friend's son had joined the army. He only wished that William Henry had asked his advice before this. Now it was too late. Frontier army life would be desolate and dangerous, and William Henry did not look strong enough for it. It would be hard enough just to stay alive, much less earn a good living. William Henry listened politely, although he didn't agree with Morris. He felt that his fortune might well be made on the other side of the Appalachians.

Harrison's guardian, Philadelphia financier Robert Morris

Now Philadelphia, Morris, and medical school seemed very far away. The soldiers rounded a bend and saw Fort Pitt ahead and somewhat below them. The rough log fort sat on a jagged point of land, with the Allegheny River flowing by on one side and the Monongahela on the other. Where the two rivers met, the Ohio River sprang up with a roar. Fort Pitt seemed very small and rough compared to its splendid natural surroundings. But as Ensign Harrison would discover, Fort Pitt shone in comparison with Fort Washington, the two-year-old wilderness outpost that was the soldiers' final destination.

A part of Fort Pitt, which grew into the city of Pittsburgh, Pennsylvania

The men didn't take time to rest at Fort Pitt. They put down their backpacks, picked up their axes, and began to build flatboats. The Ohio River would provide the smoothest and fastest road to Fort Washington. The flat-boats, soon ready, were nothing more than big oblong boxes, twenty feet wide and much longer. Clumsy as they looked, they could carry huge loads of heavy supplies— food, gunpowder, weapons, and even livestock. The soldiers loaded the flatboats and poled them out into the strong currents of the Ohio River.

A flatboat being guided down a river

The river ride was less exhausting than the three weeks of marching, but it was also more dangerous. The men steered the boats around islands and sunken logs, out of the shallows and away from the overhanging tree limbs. They knew to avoid the banks where Indians might ambush them. At night, meals were cooked aboard the boat, with the cooking fire set on a bed of dirt. Everyone slept on board, and guards were always posted. Ensign Harrison studied the banks each day but saw no trace of any human being. The trees grew right down to the water's edge. The shallows by the bank looked black from the shadow of overhanging branches. In the middle of the river, the water sparkled in the sunshine. So far, Harrison thought the frontier seemed beautiful but empty.

View of a new settlement in the Northwest Territory

While Harrison's party drifted down the Ohio, a twenty-three-year-old Shawnee Indian named Tecumseh was gliding swiftly through the woods north of Fort Washington. Though he moved quickly, not a twig snapped underfoot. Blue Jacket, the Shawnee war chief, had asked Tecumseh to lead a small scouting party to track the American army. The Americans at Fort Washington, led by General Arthur Saint Clair, had set out from the fort hoping to surprise and defeat the group of Indians led by Blue Jacket and other chiefs. Now Tecumseh was returning to tell Blue Jacket that their chances of doing this were slim. Tecumseh had sized Saint Clair's army at several thousand men, but numbers weren't everything. Large though it may be, the American army seemed undisciplined and unused to the wilderness.

The Americans at Fort Washington had known they were being watched, but whenever the soldiers had gone out to search for Indians, they had found no one. At night, Tecumseh and his men had made just enough noise to worry the troops and keep them awake.

Now Tecumseh and his men were hurrying back to join Blue Jacket and the others before the fighting broke out.

On November 4, 1791, the Indians attacked Saint Clair's army in the dark hour just before dawn. The Americans were taken completely by surprise. Many of the men had never fought Indians before. The wild whoops and glimpses of the warriors—with their faces painted red and black and with feathers braided in their hair—terrified the soldiers. When some of the men threw down their guns and ran, the defense caved in. The entire army ran in panic. The Indians were fast on their heels and killed over six hundred soldiers. The rest escaped only because the Indians returned to plunder the camp of horses, food, and ammunition.

Tecumseh's bravery in the battle was noticed, and he was praised around the campfires at night. The young war chief was becoming well known among the tribes of the Northwest Territory.

Tecumseh means "Crouching Panther." His tribe, the Shawnee, had originally lived in the southeastern part of the United States—in fact, "Shawnee" means *southerner*. They had left the South years before because of white settlements and moved into what is now southern Ohio. There they built several settlements, including a large one called Old Piqua. Old Piqua sprawled for miles along the

An 1819 council between Americans and a Nebraska tribe

banks of the Mad River. Wigwams and cabins stood under hardwood trees by the river banks. There were at least a thousand lodges in Old Piqua. Tecumseh was born in Old Piqua in March 1768.

The Shawnee had many neighbors—the Delaware, Miami, Sauk, Kickapoo, and Potawatomi tribes. All were Algonquian peoples, and their languages were similar. Sometimes they fought, but more often they were at peace. The women tended gardens of corn, squash, beans, and pumpkins. The men hunted in the surrounding woods, but sometimes, in the summer, they trekked west to the great plains to hunt buffalo.

George Rogers Clark

When the American Revolution began, Cornstalk, who was then the Shawnee war chief, decided that the tribe would fight on neither side. Soon afterward, Cornstalk and his sons were murdered by American settlers. In retaliation, the bitter Shawnee joined the British in their battle against the American colonists. Then, in August 1780, George Rogers Clark attacked Old Piqua, killing many Indians and burning the town. Tecumseh, only twelve years old, fled with his family. This was just five months before the burning of William Henry Harrison's family home, Berkeley.

The tribe built a new village on the Miami River. Again they named it Piqua, which means "town that rises from the ashes." Tecumseh bitterly hated the whites and was eager to fight them. He got his chance when he was just fifteen, but the battle didn't turn out as he expected. As he told a friend, "I felt afraid. When I heard the war whoops and saw the blood, I ran and hid beside a log."

Tecumseh crept back to camp after the battle. Warriors were handing the scalps they had taken to the chief. The warriors circled the fire, dancing. They brandished their tomahawks and acted out their parts in the battle. Each man chanted of his brave deeds. It was not vain talk. The scalps proved their words to be true. The bravest warriors received new names. Tecumseh was miserable over his own lack of courage, although none criticized him. He vowed to fight the next time.

Tecumseh lived up to his vow many times over during the next eight years. By the time of the battle with Saint Clair, Tecumseh had proved himself a powerful fighter. Though fierce in battle, he was not cruel. He allowed no one to harm prisoners or women and children.

Besides being a fierce warrior, Tecumseh was also developing into a gifted speaker. The Shawnee had no written language, and though Tecumseh knew English, he refused to speak in any but the Shawnee language. All who heard Tecumseh speak were moved. One man, Sam Dole, said, "I have heard many great orators but I never saw one with the vocal powers of Tecumseh, or the same command of the muscles of his face. Had I been deaf, the play of his countenance would have told me what he said."

Tecumseh, chief of the Shawnee

Tecumseh would never permit a white artist to paint him, but contemporary reports say that he was handsome, tall, slim, and athletic. People noticed his hazel eyes and white, even teeth. An American officer wrote that Tecumseh was "one of the finest men I ever saw, about six feet high, straight with large fine features and altogether a daring, bold-looking fellow."

When William Henry Harrison set out on flatboat down the Ohio River, he had never heard of the Shawnee warrior named Tecumseh. But the young ensign saw the results of Tecumseh's work when he reached Fort Washington. There, the bloodied and exhausted survivors of Saint Clair's army told Harrison all he needed to know of the Shawnee who would become his adversary.

A 1790 drawing of Fort Washington, later to become Cincinnati, Ohio

That dark November afternoon at Fort Washington proved to be just the first of many times that Harrison's and Tecumseh's paths would cross. Many years later, Harrison would write about Tecumseh as "one of those uncommon geniuses, which spring up occasionally to produce revolution and overturn the established order of things. If it were not for the vicinity of the United States, he would perhaps be the founder of an Empire that would rival in glory that of Mexico or Peru. No difficulties deter him. His activity and industry supply the want of letters. For four years he has been in constant motion. You see him today on the Wabash and in a short time you hear of him on the shores of Lake Erie, or Michigan, or the banks of the Mississippi, and wherever he goes, he makes an impression favourable to his purpose."

An engraving of William Henry Harrison

Chapter 2

Fallen Timbers

The Black Swamp was well named. The soldiers waded knee deep in black murky water. The whine of mosquitos was constant. William Henry Harrison steered his stallion Fearnaught to higher ground. Despite the steamy heat, wet feet, and biting insects, the soldiers were in good spirits. Finally they were moving north into Indian country.

The year was 1794. Harrison, now twenty-one years old, had lived on the frontier for almost three years. Soon after he arrived, he realized that the hardest part of frontier life was not the danger but the boredom. Fort Washington was a small log fort built on a steep hill overlooking the Ohio River. The soldiers lived in small, dark blockhouses inside the fort. Cincinnati, which lay outside the fort, was small and very quiet. Harrison quickly noticed that many soldiers drank too much and that duels were often fought from sheer boredom. Observing all this, Harrison resolved to spend his spare time reading.

He returned to Virginia only once—when his mother, Elizabeth, died in 1793. While there, Harrison sold his Virginia lands to his brother Benjamin. In return he received a tract of land in Kentucky and some money. William Henry Harrison had chosen the West.

After his visit to Virginia, Harrison was anxious to return to army life. Military life was changing. Saint Clair's defeat had shocked Congress into authorizing a larger army with General "Mad" Anthony Wayne in command. Wayne had earned his nickname with his wild bravery during the Revolution. Now he was forty-eight years old, still brave, but much more careful. He drilled his army endlessly to ready them for wilderness war.

Harrison was now a lieutenant and Wayne's third aide-de-camp. As a member of the regiment known as the First Sub-Legion, Harrison was in the good company of such men as Meriwether Lewis and William Clark—who would later become famous for their travels in the West. The soldiers wore white vests and breeches, blue coats trimmed in red, and large-brimmed leather hats. Harrison's unit decorated their hats with bearskin crests.

The army was heading for the Maumee River rapids. The British Fort Miami was there, near present-day Toledo, Ohio. From this fort the British were supplying the Indians with guns and with promises of help in their struggles against the Americans.

Harrison admired Wayne's caution during the march. Mounted men scouted for Indians in all directions. The soldiers were ordered to march in long, spread-out columns so Indians couldn't surprise and surround the entire army. Every night, the men felled trees and built a large breastwork of logs to conceal all three thousand men. It was tiring work at the end of a day's march, but Wayne insisted that it be done no matter how far the men had marched.

Above: General "Mad" Anthony Wayne and the capture of Stony Point, New York, during the Revolution.   Below: Explorers William Clark (left) and Meriwether Lewis (right)

One night, a handful of Indian warriors came riding through the forest. Their horses' manes and tails were neatly combed and braided Indian-style. Tecumseh and his scouts were on their way north to join Chief Blue Jacket near Fort Miami. Tecumseh had a good feel for Wayne's army. Unlike Saint Clair's army three years earlier, these men appeared alert and obedient. No one straggled behind. There were many scouts and guards. This army would not be a weak foe.

The Indians had formed a high regard for Wayne as an enemy. As Chief Little Turtle said, "The Americans are now led by a chief who never sleeps. He is like a deadly blacksnake."

On August 20, 1794, Wayne's scouts reported that the Indians were only five miles away, near the British fort. The soldiers prepared to fight by dropping their heavy packs on the ground, then marching on in silence. Harrison's heart pounded as he rode next to General Wayne. This was his first real battle. As aide-de-camp, he would carry the general's orders to the men. He and Fearnaught would be obvious targets. But there was another reason for Harrison's excitement. It was his own battle plan that would be followed today. General Wayne had liked his suggestions for marching and battle positions better than those of men with much greater wartime experience. It was an exciting day for the young lieutenant.

Meanwhile, the Indians had taken up their positions in a field filled with recently uprooted trees. Until the night before, there had been 1,300 Indians hiding among the fallen timbers. But a severe thunderstorm had driven many of them to abandon their positions and seek shelter in an Indian camp several miles away. Now Tecumseh was left with just over 400 warriors to do battle with Wayne's army of 3,000.

The Indians did have the element of surprise on their side, however. Their ambush threw the first line of Wayne's horsemen into confusion. But the cavalry soon regrouped. Charging the Indians from two sides, they passed right through them to block their escape. The Indians were trapped between the infantry in front and the cavalry in back.

Tecumseh gathered a group of close friends and fierce fighters around him. He fought ceaselessly until his rifle jammed and became useless. Undaunted, he slashed out with his knife until a friend handed him another rifle.

Harrison, too, was in the thick of the battle, carrying Wayne's orders back and forth and encouraging the men to fight courageously. Amazingly, he was not hurt. Later, he gave the credit to Fearnaught, saying, "My gallant steed bore me onward with such rapidity that I escaped unhurt."

The Battle of Fallen Timbers lasted only forty minutes. The Indians, outnumbered and outgunned, finally gave up the fight and ran for cover to Fort Miami. But when the British saw them coming, they slammed the gates shut. Tecumseh, who lost a brother in the battle, could never forgive or forget that "when we retreated to our father's fort, the gates were shut against us."

Harrison was commended for his bravery at the Battle of Fallen Timbers. A major said, "where the hottest of the action raged, there we could see Harrison giving the order."

Another officer said that if Harrison "continues a military man, he will be a second Washington."

A year after the Battle of Fallen Timbers—on August 3, 1795—the Treaty of Greenville was signed by ninety-two Indian chiefs and twenty-seven American officers, including Lieutenant Harrison. In addition to agreeing to live in peace and release any prisoners, the Indians gave up their lands in southern, central, and eastern Ohio. In return, they were paid $20,000 in goods and were promised antoher $9,500 over the following years.

Tecumseh took no part in the peace council at Greenville. He refused to sign a treaty that gave away huge tracts of tribal land for some blankets and a few kegs of rum. He knew that nothing, certainly not the sum of money that was offered, could pay for the loss of those lands. Though Tecumseh was still not a major Shawnee chief, his beliefs earned him a growing band of followers. After the Greenville Treaty was signed, he and this band left the white man's land and headed west. The old homeland was gone.

Back at Fort Washington, Harrison had a new preoccupation—Anna Symmes. He thought of her often and saw her when he could. It wasn't easy. Although her home was only sixteen miles away in North Bend, her father let Harrison know that he was not welcome there. Judge John Cleves Symmes didn't want a soldier for a son-in-law. But Judge Symmes hadn't counted on Harrison's determination. One cold November day, the judge returned home from a trip to find his daughter gone. She and Harrison had married while he was away, and she now lived with her new husband at Fort Washington.

Above: The Battle of Fallen Timbers
Below: Negotiating the Treaty of Greenville

The frontier was a small place, and it wasn't long before the judge met Harrison in public. When Judge Symmes bellowed, "How do you expect to support my daughter?" Harrison coolly responded, "My sword is my means of support, sir!" The judge was pleased with Harrison's manner and his pride. Over time, the two men became fast friends.

The Harrisons' first child, Betsy, was born in September 1796. There would be nine other children. Harrison soon realized that his army pay did not go far toward the support of a family. When President John Adams appointed him the secretary of the Northwest Territory in 1798, the Harrisons were overjoyed. The job paid $1,200 a year. Harrison quit the army and bought a farm at North Bend.

By 1799, there were so many people living in the Northwest Territory that the area qualified for second-class government. This was a big step on the way to statehood. The territory could now have its own elected house of representatives, a council, and a delegate in Congress. Harrison was determined to be that delegate. When he let this be known, he was visited by some important leaders of the Republican party. These men felt that public land was being sold in a way that was unfair to the common people. If Harrison would agree to work to change the land laws once he was in office, the Republicans would support him. Harrison's view was similar to theirs. He agreed to be their candidate.

The election, though very close, was a victory for Harrison. At age twenty-seven, he was off to attend Congress, which then met in Philadelphia. The city, with its neat line

Public buildings in Philadelphia

of brick rowhouses, shady streets, and bustling shops, impressed Harrison after his years in a rough frontier town. Once in Congress, he lived up to his promise and worked to change the land laws.

Public land was being sold in 640-acre chunks. Since settlers couldn't afford these large tracts, they were bought by speculators. The speculators then divided the land into many smaller pieces and sold them to settlers for large profits. Harrison wrote a law that would let land be sold in 320-acre chunks. Settlers could make a small down payment and pay off the rest in four years. The law passed and was known as the Harrison Land Law.

BY WILLIAM HENRY HARRISON,

GOVERNOR OF THE INDIANA TERRITORY, AND SUPERINTENDANT OF INDIAN AFFAIRS.

WHEREAS *Alexis Picard* ———— of the county of *Knox* ——— ha*s* made application for permiſſion to trade with the *Miami & other* nation of Indians, and ha*s* given bond according to law, for the due obſervance of all the laws and regulations for the government of the trade with Indians that now are, or hereafter may be enacted and eſta-bliſhed, licenſe is hereby granted to the ſaid *Alexis Picard* ———— to trade with the ſaid *Miami & other* nation, at their town *at or near Fort Wayne*, and there to ſell, barter and exchange with the individuals of the ſaid nation, all manner of goods, wares and merchandizes, conformably to the laws and regulations aforeſaid; but under this expreſs condition and reſtriction, that the ſaid *Alexis Picard* ſhall not, by *himſelf his* ſervants, agents or factors, carry or cauſe to be carried to the hunting camps of the Indians of ſaid nation, any ſpecies of goods or merchandize whatſoever, and more eſpecially ſpirituous liquors of any kind; nor ſhall barter or exchange the ſame, or any of them, in any quantity whatever, on pain of forfeiture of this licenſe, and of the goods, wares and merchandize, and of the ſpirituous liquors which may have been carried to the ſaid camps, contrary to the true intent and meaning hereof, and of having *his* bond put in ſuit: and the Indians of the ſaid nation are at full liberty to ſeize and confiſcate the ſaid liquors ſo carried, and the owner or owners ſhall have no claim for the ſame, either upon the ſaid nation, or any individual thereof, nor upon the United States.

This licenſe to continue in force for one year, unleſs ſooner revoked.

GIVEN under my hand and ſeal, the *twenty firſt* day of *november*, in the year of our Lord one thouſand eight hundred and *three*

Willm Henry Harrison

A license allowing a white trader to trade with Indian tribes

In 1799, Congress divided the Northwest Territory into two parts. The eastern part was present-day Ohio. The western part would become Indiana, Illinois, Michigan, and Wisconsin. This huge area was called the Indiana Territory. Its capital was the small town of Vincennes, Indiana. President Adams appointed Harrison governor of the Indiana Territory.

The new governor arrived in Vincennes in January of 1801. His family would join him in the spring. The little town nestled on the banks of the Wabash River in the middle of rolling hills. Harrison felt that the beautiful surroundings deserved a splendid house. He began to build Grouseland, a brick mansion modeled after his childhood home of Berkeley.

Harrison's Grouseland mansion in Vincennes, Indiana

The Grouseland mansion would not be finished for years. Once built, it had thirteen rooms and four chimneys. The walls were eighteen inches thick. The rooms were filled with handsome woodwork and carved mantels. During the War of 1812, Harrison added an underground tunnel through which his family could escape an attack. From Grouseland, he governed the Indiana Territory.

Chapter 3

Governor of Indian Lands

The biggest job the new governor faced was keeping peace between the Indians and the settlers, who were mostly of French descent. It seemed odd to Harrison that this involved protecting the Indians from the settlers more often than not. In a letter to Secretary of War Henry Dearborn, Harrison wrote of the local chiefs' complaints that "their people have been killed, their lands settled on, their young men made drunk and cheated." Harrison closed his letter by saying, "Of the truth of these charges, I am well convinced."

Many Indians were killed by the settlers, but few of their murderers were ever punished. Some murderers fled the area. Those who didn't were brought to trial, but inevitably they were found not guilty in a matter of minutes by all-white juries, even when the evidence against them was very strong. Although Harrison was struck by the unfairness of this, he could do little more than make sure that trials were indeed held. No one could force a jury to convict a man.

Opposite page: An engraving of William Henry Harrison

Settlers also invaded Indian hunting grounds to hunt game. Often they took only the fur or hide and left the meat to rot. Greed depleted the forests of game. The Indians were forced to range farther and farther to find enough food to feed their families.

Harrison could see that the Indians suffered in other ways from close contact with American settlers. The tribes had no resistance to the diseases brought by the settlers. And they could not tolerate the whiskey that traders gave them in exchange for their furs.

Harrison tried hard to keep the peace between Indians and whites. He forbade hunting and settling on Indian lands. He attempted to stop the sale of whiskey to the Indians, and he never stopped trying to bring murderers to justice. None of his efforts was very successful.

Harrison was a decent man in a difficult position. Much as he sympathized with the Indians, he also represented the U.S. government—and the U.S. land policy toward the Indian tribes was simple. President Thomas Jefferson wanted the U.S. to extend west all the way to the Mississippi River.

To achieve this, Jefferson instructed Harrison to purchase all of the Indian land that he could through treaties. The Indians, according to Jefferson, should be encouraged to go into debt, since they would then become willing to sell their lands. Nineteenth-century Americans were far from seeing this as unfair. They were proud of the fact that they were buying the land and not just taking it by force. They were sure that they were bringing progress and civilization to the Indians.

Harrison hoped that the Indians would begin to farm. Then they wouldn't need huge tracts of land for hunting grounds. They could live in smaller farming settlements instead. He told the tribes, "Your Father, the President, wishes you to assemble your scattered warriors and to form towns and villages . . . he will cause you to be furnished with horses, cattle, hogs." The message was clear. The Indians could either farm or be pushed west.

But it wasn't so simple for the Indians to change from a life of roaming the woods to a life spent farming a patch of land. Indian men were brought up to hunt and fight. Only women tended garden patches. They could change their ways over a long period of time, but there was no time. Huge numbers of settlers were pouring into the territory. In 1800, there were fewer than 3,000 white American settlers in Indiana. By 1816, there would be 70,000. The Indians had little reason to like the settlers, or to want to stay and farm next to them. As long as there were good hunting grounds to the west, many Indians preferred to sell their lands and move away from the settlers. And so the selling of tribal land went on. By 1808, Harrison had bought nearly all of present-day Illinois and Indiana.

At this same time, everyone along the frontier was hearing about the Prophet. Harrison didn't like what he heard. The Prophet was a Shawnee who preached that all of the Indians must return to the old ways. He commanded his followers to hold onto their lands and to give up whiskey and white men's clothes and food. The Prophet, Harrison reflected, was a potential troublemaker. He decided to discredit the Prophet before the Indian became too powerful.

The Prophet was none other than Tecumseh's younger brother. The boy was given the name Lalawethika, which means "Him with Open Mouth." Lalawethika grew up overshadowed by his older brother. Tecumseh was handsome. Lalawethika was homely even before he lost an eye in an accident with an arrow. Tecumseh was a great hunter and athlete. Lalawethika seemed hopelessly lazy. As a man, Lalawethika drank too much, spending entire days in a stupor, sprawled outside his lodge. The members of the tribe considered him to be absolutely worthless. Then Lalawethika had a vision. Overnight, he changed. He never drank again. He began to preach. To show that he had become a new man, he took a new name—Tenskwatawa, which means "I Am the Door." But he soon became known as the Prophet.

Harrison wrote to the Delaware Indians, whose young men seemed particularly charmed by the Prophet: "Who is this pretended Prophet who dares to speak in the name of the great Creator? Demand of him some proof . . . some miracle. . . . If he really is a prophet, ask him to cause the sun to stand still, the moon to alter its course, the rivers to cease to flow."

The Prophet heard of the challenge and accepted. He asked his followers to gather late in the morning of June 16, 1806, to watch him ask the Great Spirit to blacken the sun. The canny Prophet knew that there would be a solar eclipse then.

June 16 was a clear, sunny day. The solar eclipse would be all the more impressive. Wearing flowing robes, the Prophet stood solemnly in a circle of followers, outside his lodge. At half past eleven, he pointed dramatically at the sky and asked the Great Spirit to blacken the sun. The moon crossed in front of the sun and the sky darkened. All present were awestruck. The Indians begged the Prophet to restore the sun, which he did with great fanfare.

When Harrison heard of this, he was annoyed. He had underestimated the Prophet and the Prophet had won the first round. Harrison wrote a letter to the Shawnees. "My children, this business must be stopped," he said firmly.

It was not stopped. In spring 1808, the Prophet's party built a new village where the Wabash and Tippecanoe Rivers met, called Prophetstown. It was only a hundred miles north of Vincennes. Harrison worried that, at high water, the Indians could reach Vincennes by canoe much faster than a soldier or scout could ride there to warn the town of their coming.

Tecumseh, meanwhile, had become convinced that the Indians must join together to form a united Indian nation. Working together, they might be strong enough to hold off the waves of white settlers. Over the next several years, he threw himself into making his dream a reality. He began traveling to speak to all the tribes of his vision of an Indian nation. He visited the Winnebago, Menominee, Kickapoo, Miami, Delaware, and Potawatomi tribes, traveling through the Northwest Territory as far west as Wisconsin. He approached the Ottawa Indians of Canada and the Chickasaw, Choctaw, and Creek Indians of the southern United States. Tecumseh's message was clear: "These lands are ours. The Great Spirit has appointed this place for us and here we will remain."

OFFICIAL ACCOUNT

Of Gov. Harrison's battle with the Indians.

The following message from the President of the United States, enclosing Gov. Harrison's two letters to the Secretary at War, on the subject of the late engagement with the Indians on the Wabash, was laid before Congress on Thursday last.

To the Senate and House of Representatives of the United States.

I lay before Congress two letters received from Gov. Harrison of the Indians Territory, reporting the particulars and the issue of the expedition under his command, of which notice was taken in my communication of November 5.

While it is deeply lamented that so many valuable lives have been lost in the action which took place on the 7th ult. Congress will see with satisfaction the dauntless spirit and fortitude victoriously displayed by every description of the troops engaged, as well as the collected firmness which distinguished their commander on an occasion requiring the utmost exertions of valour and discipline.

It may reasonably be expected that the good effects of this critical defeat and dispersion of a combination of savages which appears to have been spreading to a greater extent, will be experienced not only in a cessation of the murders and depredations committed on our frontier, but in the prevention of any hostile incursions otherwise to have been apprehended.

The families of those brave and patriotic citizens who have fallen in this severe conflict, will doubtless engage the attention of Congress.

JAMES MADISON.

Washington, Dec. 18, 1811

Chapter 4

Hero of Tippecanoe

The Indiana Territory was shrinking. Michigan had split away to become a state in 1803. In 1808, Congress lopped off Illinois and Wisconsin. The settlers who were left wanted to live in a state, too, but there were not enough free white males in the Indiana Territory to qualify it for statehood. New settlers were bypassing the Indiana Territory and moving on to Illinois and Wisconsin, where more land had been opened up for sale to settlers. Most of the Indiana Territory, on the other hand, still belonged to the Indians.

Governor Harrison wanted to buy up this land from the Indians. Then settlers would have a reason to choose the Indiana Territory as a home. In the summer of 1809 he sent messengers calling the chiefs of all the area tribes to a meeting in Fort Wayne—all the chiefs except Tecumseh. In September, Harrison rode the 350 miles to Fort Wayne. Fourteen hundred Indians were there.

All day long, there were speeches. When it was Harrison's turn to speak, he pointed out that game was becoming scarce in the area. The days of fur trapping were over because the price of furs had fallen off sharply in Europe. If the Indians sold their lands, they would have the money to buy horses and cows. They could farm, and would no longer have to depend on hunting or fur trading for their living. Every evening, Harrison visited the camps of the tribes, talking to the chiefs, restating his points, answering questions, and smoothing the way for a land sale. Finally, a deal was made. The United States got three million new acres of land at a low price. Harrison wrote that this "bargain is a better one for the United States than any that has been made by me for lands south of the Wabash."

Tecumseh soon heard of the new treaty and was furious. Many young warriors from other tribes were also angry. The chiefs who signed the treaty had all received fine gifts of clothing and weapons. The young warriors felt betrayed by their leaders. Prophetstown was soon swollen with the arrival of many such angry young men.

Harrison heard that the Indians in Prophetstown were preparing for war. To forestall it, he invited the Prophet, through a messenger, to come to Vincennes and discuss the Fort Wayne Treaty. Tecumseh decided that he would see Harrison instead. He said to Harrison's messenger: "The Great Spirit said he gave this great island to his red children. He placed the whites on the other side of the big water, they were not content with their own. . . . They have driven us from the sea to the lakes, we can go no farther."

Tecumseh on his way to his meeting with Harrison

Tecumseh reached Vincennes on a Saturday night in August 1810. Eighty canoes of painted warriors were with him. On Tuesday he went to meet Harrison. Harrison was sitting on a chair on his veranda at Grouseland, reading a book while he waited for Tecumseh. Chairs were set out under a canopy on the lawn. After the men greeted each other, Harrison pointed out the chairs. Tecumseh declined to sit on one, saying, "The earth is my mother—on her bosom I will recline."

The moment of crisis in the meeting between Tecumseh and Harrison

Tecumseh opened the meeting by protesting the recent treaty signed at Fort Wayne. "Sell a country! Why not sell the air, the clouds and the great sea, as well as the earth? Did not the Great Spirit make them all for the use of his children?" Harrison defended the treaty by saying that it was signed by all of the chiefs. In response, Tecumseh warned that there would be war if the lands sold in the Fort Wayne Treaty were not returned. At one point, Tecumseh became so angry that he jumped to his feet, calling Harrison a liar. The Indians unsheathed their tomahawks. Soldiers readied their muskets. Then Harrison calmly announced that the meeting was over for the day. He turned on his heel and strode back toward his home. Everyone put away their weapons. The danger was over.

Harrison and Tecumseh met again, but no problems were resolved. Tecumseh could not persuade Harrison to give back the treaty lands. Harrison could not placate the Shawnee's anger. Harrison knew that he had a powerful foe. He wrote that he now understood that Tecumseh, not the Prophet, was "the great man of the party."

Winter passed. In the spring of 1811, Harrison heard that the Indians were again preparing for war. Once more he invited Tecumseh to Vincennes, asking him to bring only thirty warriors with him. Tecumseh came—with three hundred warriors. The townspeople were afraid that the Indians would attack the town. To make the Indians believe that there were more soldiers than there actually were, Harrison paraded the same three companies of soldiers through the streets again and again. Tecumseh, seeing the town bristling with troops, felt it was fortunate that so many warriors had chosen to travel with him.

When the men met, Harrison angrily asked why Tecumseh had brought so many men with him. Tecumseh answered that he had invited only twenty-four, but that the rest had come along because they wanted to. The meeting was short and tense. Tecumseh revealed that he was traveling south to unite the southern tribes. Would Harrison defer settlement on the treaty lands until his return? Tecumseh wanted to talk to President James Madison himself about the treaty. "As the great chief over the mountains is to decide the matter, I hope the Great Spirit will put sense enough in his head to order you to give up those lands. It is true, he may sit in his fine house and drink his wine, while you and I have to fight it out."

As soon as Tecumseh had left for the South, Harrison began preparations to destroy Prophetstown in his absence. War with the Indians was now inevitable, thought Harrison. Far better to crush Prophetstown while Tecumseh was away than to wait for him to return from the South, perhaps with more warriors than before.

Harrison gathered a thousand men. On September 26, 1811, the army set out. Harrison wore a fringed hunting shirt and a large ostrich plume in the brim of his beaver fur hat. The U.S. government knew that Harrison had an army on the move. However, President Madison had been told by Secretary of War William Eustis that Harrison was conducting a peaceful march through the lands just purchased from the Indians. Soon the army left the treaty lands and began to march through Indian lands. Although he had no authorization to do so, Harrison hoped to provoke a fight and destroy Prophetstown once and for all.

The Prophet had promised Tecumseh that he would not fight in his brother's absence. With that in mind, he sent messengers to find Harrison's army and negotiate. The messengers traveled down the east side of the Wabash River, missing the army completely. Unbeknownst to the Indians, Harrison had already crossed his men to the west side of the river.

Although the Indians wished to avoid a fight if possible, they were not afraid of one. The Potawatomi chief Shabbona, a good friend of Tecumseh, was optimistic about any battle. He said of the approaching army, "Their hands are soft, their faces are white. . . . One half of them are calico peddlers. The other half can only shoot squirrels."

On November 6, the army camped near the mouth of the Tippecanoe River, just a mile from Prophetstown. Chief White Horse and some of his warriors rode out from the village to meet Harrison. Harrison trotted his gray mare forward. After White Horse sternly pointed out that the Americans were on Indian land, both sides agreed to talk the next day. Then White Horse and his men returned to their town, and the army encamped for the night.

In Prophetstown that evening, the Indians held a council. After much discussion, they decided it was best to attack before the army attacked them. The Prophet himself would not fight, but he agreed to use all of his magic powers to help the Indians.

Throughout the chilly night, there were spells of drizzly rain. Between showers, the moon shone through a cover of ragged clouds. Under this cover of darkness, the Indians inched forward through the wet grass on their bellies. They hoped to be in among the soldiers before they were noticed, but an alert guard spotted one of them and fired his rifle. The quiet night was split by war cries and gunfire. The battle began at 4:00 A.M. on November 7, 1811.

Harrison jumped into his boots and rushed from his tent to find his gray mare. But in the confusion he mounted a bay horse instead. His aide took the gray horse and was instantly shot from the saddle. The Indians knew Harrison's mare and had shot for its rider.

The battle raged for over two hours. The Indians had 450 warriors to fight Harrison's army of 1,000. They had counted on surprise to help them, but the alert sentry changed all that. Defeat seemed certain.

Once again, Harrison had proved his courage. He always seemed to be where the fighting was hardest. At dawn he ordered a mounted charge, and the Indians retreated into a swamp where the horses could not follow. The Battle of Tippecanoe was over. The Prophet and his Indians abandoned the area, and Harrison's army burned Prophetstown before marching back to Vincennes.

Tippecanoe, as the battle was named, made Harrison famous. It would someday make him president. Yet he knew that he had had no orders allowing him to enter Indian country and provoke a fight. Harrison himself recognized this when he said, "I have indeed for some time expected to be called to Washington to answer for my invasion of the Indian country."

Tecumseh first learned of Tippecanoe when he rounded a bend of the Wabash and saw blackened ashes where Prophetstown had once stood. "I stood upon the ashes of my own home. . . . I summoned the spirits of the braves who had fallen in their brave attempt to protect their homes from the grasping invader. . . . I swore once more eternal hatred." Tecumseh found the Prophet among the Indians who had returned to rebuild the town. He grabbed his brother by the hair, shook him, and shouted in his face. Why did the Prophet not avoid this fight?

Tippecanoe was a major setback for Tecumseh. After the battle, he saw that he must work even harder for his dream of a united Indian nation. An opportunity quickly arose. On June 18, 1812, the U.S. declared war against Great Britain. Tecumseh offered his services as an ally to the British in Canada.

Opposite page: Harrison's men charge
during the Battle of Tippecanoe

Chapter 5

The War of 1812

Many western Americans welcomed the War of 1812. They saw it as a chance to win Canada from the British. For years, British traders from Canada had crossed the border into the U.S. at will to trade with the Indian tribes. The Treaty of 1783, signed after the revolutionary war, gave the traders a legal right to engage in such trading. But many westerners believed that the traders urged the Indians to attack American settlers. The traders denied this. Trading, they said, was better in peacetime. They did not want fighting in the Northwest Territory.

The War of 1812 was a trade war. For years, the Napoleonic wars between Britain and France had been ruining American sea trade. In an attempt to destroy the other's trade, neither country would permit the U.S. to ship cargo to the other. To add insult to injury, British men-of-war were stopping American ships on the high seas and taking sailors by force, claiming that they were British deserters. Some were, but many were American citizens. The U.S. was angry with both Britain and France. Impressment— the taking of sailors from American ships—was the final straw. The U.S. decided to go to war against Britain.

Opposite page: A romanticized portrait of Harrison and his deeds

The impressment of an American seaman

At the start of the war, many people were enthused. Frontier Americans saw it as a chance to invade Canada. Tecumseh saw opportunity, too. If Great Britain won, the Indians, as British allies, could demand land for a separate Indian nation as part of the peace treaty. And if the British should lose? Tecumseh was a realist. "If they should not win . . . it will not be many years before our last abode and our last hunting ground will be taken from us and the remnants of the different tribes . . . will all be driven . . . toward the setting sun," he said soberly.

William Hull

Harrison saw a chance to lead men again, for he enjoyed soldiering. But to his disappointment, another man, General William Hull, was given the job of commander of the American army in the West. In July, Hull marched north to Detroit with an army of three thousand. The key British forts of Malden and Amherstburg lay within Canada not far from Detroit, and Hull intended to invade. Harrison thought that the invasion was premature. He felt that it was useless to invade until the U.S. could control the Great Lakes. Until then, any American soldiers in Canada would be cut off from supplies and reinforcements.

General Issac
Brock (1769-1812),
commander of the
British forces

Hull's invasion went badly. Once in Canada, he heard that Fort Malden had been reinforced and that the British and Indians had captured the island fort of Michilimackinac, on Lake Michigan. Fearful that thousands of hostile warriors would soon be descending on him, he lost his nerve and ordered a retreat to Detroit. His soldiers hated to retreat without even a fight. Tecumseh's Indians captured some letters written by soldiers in the retreating army. The letters all complained that Hull was a coward. Tecumseh had not seen much fighting spirit in Hull, either, but the letters confirmed it. Tecumseh took the letters to the British commander, General Isaac Brock. The British leader and the Indian leader decided to march on Detroit. Hull, they thought, would be an easy foe.

Hull felt somewhat reassured when his army reached the fort at Detroit. Detroit had a much better than average frontier fort. It was thick-walled and surrounded by deep ditches, and it fairly bristled with guns. At Detroit, Hull had the advantages of a strong fort and an army of eager, well-trained soldiers. In his own mind, however, Hull was a beaten man. He thought only of defeat and an Indian massacre.

When Brock and Tecumseh appeared and threatened to invade, Hull surrendered Detroit, his army, and all of his supplies without fighting. The war was off to a miserable start for the United States.

After Detroit, Hull was in disgrace, and President Madison was looking about for a new commander for the army. In September 1812, Harrison was given command of the American army in the Northwest Territory. The soldiers were pleased to follow Harrison, whom they knew to be both brave and kind. As one soldier said, "Harrison, with a look, can awe or convince or persuade." Harrison himself was thrilled to command the army, but his job was a tough one. His orders were to protect the entire frontier, to win Detroit back, and to invade Canada.

Much as Harrison would have liked to march to Detroit immediately, moving such a large army was not that easy. The soldiers needed supplies that were hard to obtain. There was not enough food or clothing for all of the men. The prices on supplies were high, and many supplies that were sent by army contractors were of poor quality. Harrison wrote, "I am all out of patience with the rascally contractors."

Fort Harrison, built near Terre Haute, Indiana, in 1811

The weather was also a problem. All through the autumn it rained, so that supply wagons were continually bogged down. The supplies were finally shifted to boats. But then winter arrived, seemingly overnight. It turned bitterly cold. The supply boats were caught fast in the middle of frozen streams and rivers.

In December, the usually optimistic Harrison realized that this war would not be over quickly. He resigned the governorship of the Indiana Territory. He would concentrate on being a good commander of the army.

Indians allied with the French against the British and Americans during the French and Indian War of 1756 to 1763.

Once the army was on the road, misfortune struck. A General Winchester had charge of part of the army. He was supposed to report to Harrison, but he took his men to the small village of Frenchtown on the Raisin River, in southern Michigan, without telling Harrison. Winchester set up camp carelessly. He picked open ground and did not post enough guards. The troops were not ordered to dig in or erect breastworks. Winchester ignored reports that the enemy was coming. Sure enough, the Americans were attacked by British and Indian forces in the early morning hours of a bitterly cold January day. Many men were killed; the rest were captured. Many of those captured were later killed by Indian tribesmen. Harrison was furious that so many lives were lost out of carelessness.

In February, Harrison's men built Fort Meigs at the Maumee Rapids near the site of the Battle of Fallen Timbers. The army wintered there in the large, strong fort. In late April, British gunboats appeared on Lake Erie. British soldiers, a thousand of them, poured out on shore on the other side of the Maumee River. Tecumseh soon appeared with twelve hundred Indians. They had come around the lake by land. Tecumseh and the new British commander, Henry Proctor, rode horseback up to the edge of the river to study the fort on the other side. The fort looked strong, but the British and Indian forces outnumbered the Americans, and the British had brought some cannon.

Harrison was happy to see the enemy. He said, "My wishes are that they attack us here." Tecumseh, on the other hand, had to work hard to encourage his men to stay for a siege. The Indians disliked this type of warfare. They favored quick battles, not long sieges. Tecumseh tried to lure Harrison out of the fort with taunting notes. He wrote to Harrison, "You hide behind logs and in the earth like a ground hog." Harrison, who knew that he was in a good position, did not reply.

Finally, on May 1, the first shots were fired. The British pounded the fort with their big guns for three days. Then Proctor demanded that Harrison surrender. Harrison replied, "Assure your general . . . that he will never have the fort surrendered on any terms." When Harrison received reinforcements, Proctor saw that it would not be so easy after all to take Fort Meigs. Harrison was not another Hull. On May 9, the British sailed away. The Indians withdrew, too. The first Battle of Fort Meigs had ended.

Tecumseh at Fort Meigs

Oliver Hazard Perry at the Battle of Lake Erie

The British had controlled the Great Lakes from the beginning of the war. At Erie, Pennsylvania, Commodore Oliver Hazard Perry was struggling to put together a fleet for the U.S. His small fleet was undermanned, and he was bottled up in port by the more powerful British fleet. Perry could not get his ships out of port until the British left. Finally, one day in late July, the British fleet sailed out of sight. Perry had no idea how long they would be gone. But it could be his only chance to leave the port of Erie for a long time.

The American crews rushed into action. The smaller boats cleared the harbor easily, but the larger ships were grounded on a large sandbar at the mouth of the harbor. The ships had to be made lighter. Cannon and heavy supplies were removed. Slowly, carefully, the ships were coaxed over the sandbar. Once they were clear, the cannons were remounted in a great hurry. No sooner was the fleet out of harbor and reassembled than the British ships appeared on the horizon. They were too late to stop Perry. The American fleet was free of the harbor.

That night, Perry sat at his desk in the captain's quarters and wrote to Harrison: "The squadron is not more than half manned, but as I see no prospect of receiving reinforcements, I have determined to commence. . . . My anxiety to join you is very great."

Harrison was also anxious to meet Perry. The fleet dropped anchor in Sandusky Bay on a gray, rainy day. That evening, Harrison was rowed out to the flagship, the *Lawrence*. He brought along some friendly Wyandot Indians who were so delighted by the "great canoe" that they held a war dance on deck. Harrison stayed aboard for two days, discussing the war with Perry. The men liked each other. Both were brave and optimistic. Perry would soon prove himself to be an unusually tenacious man. He never quit, even when defeat seemed certain.

Perry was bothered by a shortage of boat crews. Vowing to help, Harrison returned to Fort Meigs and called for volunteers to assist Perry. One hundred men stepped forward. They were quickly taken to the fleet and given crash lessons in seamanship.

Perry hoped that the British fleet would attack him. If he won, the American fleet could carry Harrison's army across Lake Erie to Detroit. With this in mind, he sailed out in search of the British. On September 10, 1813, Harrison, in Fort Meigs, heard the distant roar of guns on the lake. Tecumseh, who was camped on Bois Blanc Island, heard the noise, too.

At the onset of the battle, Perry had more ships than the British had. However, Perry was both outgunned and outweighed. Once the fleets sighted each other, they halted, still several miles apart. Both sides prepared for battle. Ammunition was brought out, and loose gear was stored away. The ships maneuvered into battle lines, facing each other.

The British line looked majestic: *Chippewa, Detroit* (Barclay's flagship), *Hunter, Queen Charlotte, Lady Prevost,* and *Little Belt.* Perry arranged his line so that the *Lawrence,* his flagship, would fight the *Detroit. Caledonia* lined up opposite *Hunter. Niagara* was in position to attack *Queen Charlotte.* That left four small American ships—the *Somers, Porcupine, Tigris,* and *Tripp*—to engage the two remaining men-of-war. Perry hoped that the four smaller craft could annoy *Lady Prevost* and *Little Belt* and keep them busy.

When all was ready, Perry ordered the fighting flag to be brought out. Large white letters spelled out "Don't Give Up the Ship" against a blue background. The sailors drank cups of grog. A fighting tune was played to the music of drums and fife. The battle lines moved together. Just before noon, the first shot of battle was fired.

Commodore Perry carries the "Don't Give Up the Ship" banner by rowboat from the crippled flagship *Lawrence* to the *Niagara*. From there he went on to win the Battle of Lake Erie.

The guns on the American ships had a shorter range and less power, so Perry sailed the *Lawrence* right up to the British line. The *Lawrence* had to get close to do any damage at all. The *Caledonia* sailed bravely in to grapple with the *Hunter*. But Captain Elliot, commander of the *Niagara*, hung back. He never attacked *Queen Charlotte* at all. Instead, he sailed back and forth on the edge of the battle for several hours, leaving the *Queen Charlotte* free to turn all of its guns on the *Lawrence*. The *Lawrence* was soon hopelessly damaged, with most of its men killed or wounded.

But Perry would not quit. He hauled the fighting flag into a small oarboat and had his men row him to the intact *Niagara*. There he relieved Captain Elliot of command and sailed the *Niagara* straight through the British line. He headed first for the *Detroit* and the *Queen Charlotte*. They were side by side, and Perry could fire on both at once. Within five minutes, the *Detroit* and the *Queen Charlotte* were so badly damaged that they hauled down their flags and stopped fighting. The *Niagara* turned next on the *Lady Prevost* and the *Hunter*. One by one, the British ships struck down their colors.

By 4:00 P.M., the battle was over. British officers boarded the *Niagara* to offer their swords to Perry. Barclay, the British commander, had been badly wounded just as the *Lawrence* hauled down flag and British victory seemed certain. Barclay could hardly believe that the Americans had won the battle. As he told Perry, "When I left the deck, I would not have given sixpence for your chance."

Right: General William
Henry Harrison
in his uniform

Below: The *Niagara* (right)
fires on the British
ship *Detroit* (center).

Harrison was elated to receive Perry's short message: "We have met the enemy and they are ours." Lake Erie belonged to the U.S. now. Even Tecumseh realized it. He could not understand why Proctor decided to abandon Fort Malden and retreat north into Canada. He was full of contempt for the British commander, saying, "We are sorry to see that you are getting ready to flee before you even have sight of the enemy. We must compare your conduct to a fat animal that carries its tail on its back, but, when frightened, drops it between its legs and runs."

Proctor, in turn, wrote, "I hate these savage barbarians." Goaded by Tecumseh, he finally promised to retreat only as far north as the Thames River. If Harrison followed them that far, they would stand and fight.

On the other side of the lake, Harrison and his men boarded Perry's ships in late September. As the ships sailed, Harrison spotted a soaring eagle. He took it as a sign of victory. By September 27, the men had landed less than five miles from Fort Malden. Harrison encouraged his men, saying, "Remember the River Raisin! but remember it only whilst the victory is suspended. The revenge of a soldier cannot be gratified upon a fallen enemy."

The British were still on the retreat. Tecumseh was tired of trying to inspire Proctor with some fight. When they reached the Thames River, he had to remind Proctor that he had promised to fight there. "Father," implored Tecumseh, "have a big heart!" So the British and the Indians took up positions alongside the road that ran by the banks of the river. They waited. It was the morning of October 5, 1813.

Peace of Ghent 1814. and Triumph of America

Above: A symbolic depiction of the Treaty of Ghent, ending the War of 1812
Below: Harrison and his staff at the Battle of the Thames

The death of Tecumseh at the Battle of the Thames

Harrison and his army crossed the Thames early in the day. Since the river was deep and swift, most of the army crossed in boats. The cavalry swam across on their horses. On the opposite side, they regrouped. Scouts told Harrison that the enemy was just ahead. Harrison decided to send the cavalry in first. "The American backwoodsmen ride better in the woods than any other people. A musket or rifle is no impediment," he reasoned.

It was late afternoon when Tecumseh finally heard bugles and the hoofbeat of cavalry. The riders charged, shouting, "Remember the River Raisin!" The battle cry terrified Proctor, who fled the field, leaving his army to

Another artist's rendition of Tecumseh's death

fight without him. The British defense lasted for barely fifteen minutes. But although the British surrendered after the first cavalry charge, the Indians fought on stubbornly. Tecumseh's voice lifted above the noise as he urged his men to be brave. The Americans dismounted and advanced on foot, fighting hard. Tecumseh was wounded several times, and his men were badly outgunned and outnumbered. When they finally ran out of ammunition, they threw down their guns and fought with knives and tomahawks. Suddenly, Tecumseh's voice fell silent. Demoralized, the Indians retreated, still fighting, back into the forest. Dusk settled. The Battle of the Thames was over. Harrison had won a great victory.

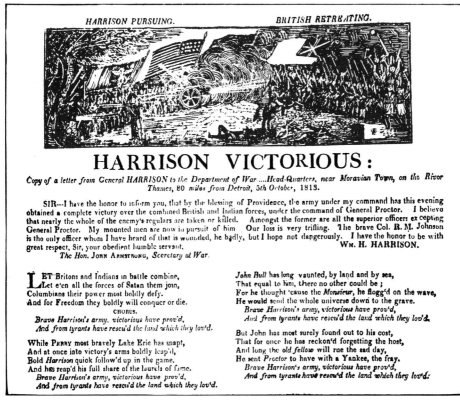

HARRISON VICTORIOUS:

Copy of a letter from General HARRISON to the Department of War ....Head-Quarters, near Moravian Town, on the River Thames, 80 miles from Detroit, 5th October, 1813.

SIR---I have the honor to inform you, that by the blessing of Providence, the army under my command has this evening obtained a complete victory over the combined British and Indian forces, under the command of General Proctor. I believe that nearly the whole of the enemy's regulars are taken or killed. Amongst the former are all the superior officers excepting General Proctor. My mounted men are now in pursuit of him. Our loss is very trifling. The brave Col. R. M. Johnson is the only officer whom I have heard of that is wounded, he badly, but I hope not dangerously. I have the honor to be with great respect, Sir, your obedient humble servant,

WM. H. HARRISON.

The Hon. JOHN ARMSTRONG, Secretary at War.

LET Britons and Indians in battle combine,
Let e'en all the forces of Satan them join,
Columbians their power most boldly defy.
And for Freedom they boldly will conquer or die.
CHORUS.
Brave Harrison's army, victorious have prov'd,
And from tyrants have rescu'd the land which they lov'd.

While PERRY most bravely Lake Erie has snapt,
And at once into victory's arms boldly leap'd,
Bold Harrison quick follow'd up in the game.
And has reap'd his full share of the laurels of fame.
Brave Harrison's army, victorious have prov'd,
And from tyrants have rescu'd the land which they lov'd.

John Bull has long vaunted, by land and by sea,
That equal to him, there no other could be ;
For he thought 'cause the Monsieur, he flogg'd on the wave,
He would send the whole universe down to the grave.
Brave Harrison's army, victorious have prov'd,
And from tyrants have rescu'd the land which they lov'd.

But John has most surely found out to his cost,
That for once he has reckon'd forgetting the host,
And long the old fellow will rue the sad day,
He sent Proctor to have with a Yankee, the fray.
Brave Harrison's army, victorious have prov'd,
And from tyrants have rescu'd the land which they lov'd.

A song written to celebrate Harrison's victory at the Thames

The next day, the Americans searched the field for the body of Tecumseh. They could not find it. For a long time afterward, the Americans were not sure that Tecumseh was in fact really killed. To this day, Tecumseh's grave has not been found. The dream of a united Indian people died with Tecumseh. It would not be many years until the tribes would be pushed "toward the setting sun."

Harrison's victory should have brought him the gratitude of the U.S. government. Instead, it made Secretary of War John Armstrong jealous. As one young ensign under Harrison's command put it, "We understand the whole matter out here. The people in Washington have got scared of Harrison's victories. They are afraid a few more might make him President! Therefore, they have determined to put him out of the way."

The U.S. Capitol after the British burned it

Armstrong started giving Harrison odd and contradictory orders. He also sent orders to Harrison's subordinates without asking Harrison's opinion. Harrison tried to work with Armstrong but, finally, resigned in disgust on May 11, 1814. Armstrong himself would be forced to resign in August 1814 after the British burned Washington as part of their war effort.

The war itself dragged on until the end of 1814, but Harrison did not participate after his resignation. At the end of the war, he was asked to help conclude a peace treaty with the Indians. The Treaty of Spring Wells, signed on September 8, 1815, restored to the tribes all of the lands and rights that they had at the outbreak of war. Nine tribes signed. The Prophet was there and also signed the treaty. Without Tecumseh, the Prophet's power to unite the Indians against the Americans was gone.

Chapter 6

From Congress to Colombia

The war had made Harrison a poorer man. His army pay of $2,400 a year had not been enough to provide for his large family, which by then included ten children. He managed only by borrowing money. No longer governor of the Indiana Territory, he returned to his log cabin at North Bend and began remodeling. He added two large wings to the cabin, enlarged the center portion of the structure, and had the entire house covered in clapboard. The small log cabin had become a comfortable, sixteen-room house.

Though not a rich man, Harrison loved to entertain, and the Harrison house was open to all. Travelers were never asked to leave—and many stayed for quite a while! Timothy Flint, a friend of the Harrisons, said, "He kept an open table to which every visitor was welcome. The table was loaded . . . especially with the different types of game." This hospitality was expensive. The Harrisons went through 365 hams alone in one year. Flint said of Harrison during this period, "His eye is brilliant. There is a good deal of ardour and vivacity in his manner."

The Harrisons' residence in North Bend, Ohio

Of course, open hospitality was common in the area. A British visitor, Frances Trollope, wrote of the hospitality of the Cincinnati area in 1832, "No one dreams of fastening a door in Western America; I was told that it would be considered an affront to the whole neighborhood." Trollope also wrote of the westerners "taking more tea, coffee, hot cake and custard, hoe cake, johnny cake, waffle cake and dodger cake, pickled peaches and preserved cucumbers, ham, turkey, hung beef, applesauce and pickled oysters than ever were prepared in any other country of the known world."

While in North Bend, Harrison heard that his critics in Washington were accusing him of profiting unfairly from the war by taking money from the army suppliers. Harrison became so annoyed by these false stories that he decided to run for Congress. If he were in Washington, he could defend himself. Not surprisingly, he was elected to the House of Representatives in 1816.

In Washington, Harrison took a small room in a boardinghouse. Washington was more of a rural town than an elegant city at this point. Grass grew in the streets and pigs wandered about. The British had burned parts of the city, including the Capitol, during the war, and repairs were not yet finished.

Harrison tried to interest Congress in a bill calling for universal military training. He believed that the U.S. had made a poor showing in the War of 1812 because of the lack of a well-trained, ready army. The bill did not pass. Harrison did, however, succeed in passing a bill to provide money for wounded soldiers and for the widows and orphans of soldiers killed in the war.

Meanwhile, a committee had investigated Harrison's war conduct and cleared him of all the charges. Harrison was greatly satisfied by this. He was, however, unhappy over his family's finances. He resigned from Congress in 1819 to go home and look after the farm in North Bend. As he said, "I am already up to the hub as deeply as I can go . . . our debts are extremely large and very pressing." To pay off some of those debts, Harrison was forced to sell some of the family's land. Despite everything, however, he managed to keep his sons in college.

Anna Symmes Harrison

In 1822, Harrison ran for the U.S. Senate, but lost in a bitterly contested race. Undaunted, he ran again in 1824 when a Senate seat became vacant, and he won. On the first day of the session, he wore a black frock coat, Kentucky jeans, and cowhide boots. A journalist singled him out: "His face is thin and oval, his complexion fair . . . his countenance serene and engaging."

Harrison missed his wife, Anna, and wrote to her of his doings: "I am obliged to devote a part of the day to exercise . . . and the rest to official business. Directly after breakfast, I have to attend on Committees or to some business at the Public offices. We generally sit now from 12 to 5 o'clock . . . it is not until some time after dinner that I can begin to answer some of my numerous correspondence which really worry me to death."

During his term in the Senate, Harrison was chairman of the military and militia committees. He worked hard and had hopes of being nominated vice-president in the next election. The nomination did not come, however, and in the spring of 1828, President Adams appointed Harrison the first U.S. minister to Colombia, in South America. The job paid $9,000 a year. Harrison accepted the job as much out of financial need as patriotic feelings. As he said, "My great object is to save a little money."

The sea passage from New York to Maracaibo, Venezuela, in the the autumn of 1828 was stormy and uncomfortable. Harrison had plenty of time to wonder about Colombia. He knew that the country was in an uproar. The land had belonged to Spain until Simón Bolívar, the Great Liberator, had wrested it from Spain.

When statesmen and generals could not agree on a constitution for the new country, Bolívar had stepped in as dictator. The United States hoped that Colombia would develop into a free, democratic nation, but no one knew what Bolivar would do. He was only forty-five, but worn out from years of fighting. When he died, what sort of government would Colombia have?

From Maracaibo, Harrison traveled 750 miles by mule train to the capital city of Bogotá, Colombia. The soaring, snow-capped mountains he crossed were unlike anything he had seen. The lives of the Colombian peasants shocked him. He saw men who were being marched off in chains to fight against their will in a war with Peru. Most of the people were dressed in rags. The children ran naked. The farms were poor, and the crops looked small to Harrison.

In February, Harrison reached Bogotá, the mountain capital. He rented a large stone mansion, but no sooner had he settled in than he heard that he had been replaced. Andrew Jackson was the new president back in Washington, and he had appointed Congressman Thomas Patrick Moore as minister to Colombia. Harrison was to stay until Moore arrived.

Harrison did not let this news ruin his stay. He had made some interesting new friends of all nationalities. He knew a British consul general, a Danish banker, a Polish nobleman, and a Mexican envoy. In his spare time, he raised vegetables. He had brought some seeds from North Bend and was curious to see if they would grow in the cool, mountainous climate of Bogotá. They did—and the produce was in great demand at official dinners.

It was plain to Harrison that the Colombians were far from free. They paid huge and unfair taxes. They could not speak badly of the government or bear arms. There were elections, but they were not secret—voters were required to sign their ballots. Those who voted against the government were likely to disappear in the middle of the night. Bolívar now wanted to be crowned emperor. The Colombian government officials disliked Harrison, who spoke out in favor of a democratic form of government at every occasion.

Moore arrived, and as Harrison was preparing to leave, trouble struck. While he was waiting for the ship *Natchez* to return from Rio de Janeiro, a General Cordova led a revolt against the government. Harrison was accused of aiding the revolt. The accusation was false, but Harrison

Simón Bolívar, South American soldier and statesman

began traveling with a bodyguard. Colombia had become a dangerous place for him. Then a close friend of his was arrested. Harrison threw himself into getting his friend released from jail and succeeded after much effort. Finally, on October 19, 1829, he was relieved to leave Bogotá. Enroute to the port of Cartagena, he heard that Cordova's revolt had failed. In Cartagena, the *Natchez* still did not appear. Anxious to get home and concerned about the safety of his party, Harrison bought their tickets home on a different ship. His days as a foreign minister were over.

A glorified rendition of Harrison's life and works

Chapter 7

The Fallen Hero

On April 15, 1830, a big sidewheeler eased up to the river dock in Cincinnati. General Harrison stepped ashore. He was home again, at last. With him he had a brilliantly-colored macaw and several exotic plants from Colombia.

Harrison's family was overjoyed to have him home again. Things had not gone well in his absence. Two of his sons had piled up huge debts. John owed $12,000, and William, Jr., more than that. Harrison himself had outstanding debts of $20,000. Altogether, it was a mountain of debt. Harrison worked hard to pay his sons' debts first, again selling land to raise money. His friends were amazed at how cheerful he remained. One said, "He is, however, of a sanguine temperament and what would, to most men, seem insurmountable obstacles . . . would to the General be disposed of very easily."

Things did not go well with Harrison's sons. In October, John died of typhoid fever, leaving a wife and six children. Harrison was brokenhearted. He and Anna took in John's family. When it became clear that William, Jr., was an alcoholic and could not provide for his family, Harrison took on that responsibility, too. Harrison was now supporting three families, his own and the families of two sons.

The year 1832 was a bleak one. Flooding along the Ohio River ruined the crops at North Bend. Weighed down by misfortunes, Harrison became seriously ill for months.

Once he was well, he hatched scheme after scheme to make money for his family. Finally, he was given a humble job as clerk of court in Cincinnati. It was better than nothing, and Harrison was grateful for the appointment. A French visitor, Michel Chevalier, spotted Harrison in Cincinnati one day and wrote: "I met with one incident in Cincinnati which I shall long remember. I had observed at the hotel table a man of about medium height, stout and muscular, and of about the age of 60 years yet with the active step and lively air of youth. I had been struck with his open and cheerful expression, the amenity of his manner and a certain air of command which appeared through his plain dress. 'That,' said my friend, 'is General Harrison, clerk of the Cincinnati court of common pleas. . . . He is now poor, with a numerous family, neglected by the federal government, although yet vigorous, because he has the independence to think for himself.' "

Oddly enough, now that Harrison's fortunes were at their lowest point, some members of the Whig party began to consider him as a candidate for the presidency. He himself chuckled over this in a letter to his old friend, General Solomon Van Rensselaer: "I am greatly aided by the support of an office humble indeed, but still honourable and lucrative. . . . But I have news still more strange to tell you. . . . Some folks are silly enough to have formed a plan to make a President of the United States out of this clerk and clodhopper."

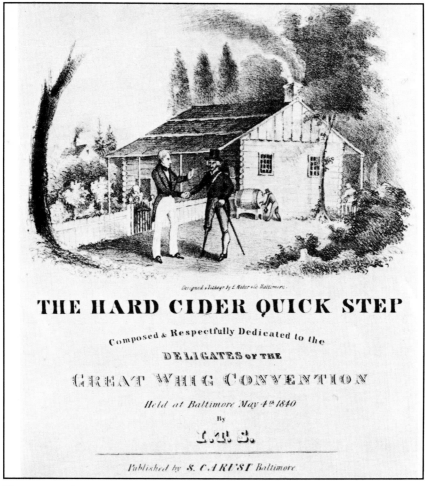

The cover of a musical composition during Harrison's campaign

Harrison was nominated by the Whig party to run for the presidency against Democratic candidate Martin Van Buren in the election of 1836. Van Buren won, but by 1838 Harrison was campaigning again, this time for the presidential election of 1840. Harrison's campaign was notable because he gave speeches on his own behalf. This was a first in America. Up until then, candidates had not given speeches because they felt it seemed self-serving. Harrison did it to prove he was neither too old nor too feeble for the strenuous job of president. From Harrison on, all presidential candidates would give campaign speeches.

A HARD ROAD TO HOE!

A cartoon showing blind Jackson leading burdened Van Buren to the White House

Harrison's running partner was John Tyler of Virginia. "Tippecanoe and Tyler, too" became Harrison's campaign slogan. Harrison himself became known as "Old Tippecanoe." His Whig campaign stayed away from issues and concentrated on emotion. The Whigs held huge torchlight rallies by night and barbeque rallies by day. There were parades with floats and banners. Harrison's supporters wore buttons and ribbons. There were hundreds of campaign songs. A Democratic newspaper editor wrote, "Some of the songs I shall never forget. They rang in my ears, morning, noon and night. Men, women and children did nothing but sing. It worried, annoyed, dumbfounded, crushed the Democrats." At one rally, a mock Indian attack was staged. The Indians were driven off, of course.

A "Log Cabin March and Quick Step" composed for Harrison's campaign

A Baltimore paper that favored Van Buren criticized Harrison as a simple backwoodsman, saying, "Give him a barrel of hard cider and a pension of two thousand a year . . . he will sit the remainder of his days in a log cabin." But the Whigs seized on this comment and the criticism backfired. Overnight, log cabins appeared everywhere—along with coonskin caps and cider barrels. There were log cabins pictured on banners and buttons. Log cabin floats appeared in parades, and the country's cider presses were never busier.

The inauguration of William Henry Harrison

The Democrats had nothing to equal the appeal of this "hard cider and log cabin" campaign. Harrison was portrayed as a western man of the people. Americans liked Harrison for his military record, his plain manner, and his simplicity. Since Harrison had not been in politics recently, no one could blame him for any recent problems. Many people, on the other hand, blamed Van Buren for the 1837 depression. Van Buren was famous for his elegant dress and manners. The Whigs portrayed Van Buren as a city dandy, in contrast with Harrison, an honest country man.

Harrison and Tyler won the election of 1840. They carried nineteen states to Van Buren's seven. Harrison was elated, but Anna, his wife, had misgivings: "I wish that my husband's friends had left him where he is, happy and contented in retirement."

Harrison fans celebrating his victory with hard cider

On January 26, 1841, Harrison stood on the deck of the steamboat *Ben Franklin* and spoke to the crowd on the Cincinnati shore as he prepared to leave for Washington. The morning was clear and cold. Harrison's words were somber: "Gentlemen and fellow-citizens; perhaps this may be the last time I may have the pleasure of speaking to you on earth or seeing you. I . . . bid you farewell." The steamboat pulled away to the cheers of the crowd.

On February 9, Harrison rode into Washington on his favorite horse, Old Whitey. It was his sixty-eighth birthday. He immediately called on his former foe, Martin Van Buren. Van Buren liked Harrison but was unsure that the new president understood the seriousness of his job. "The President is the most extraordinary man I ever saw. He does not seem to realize the vast importance of the elevation. . . . He is as tickled with the Presidency as a young woman with a new bonnet," Van Buren said later.

Harrison's vice-president, John Tyler, who succeeded him

Anna Harrison became too ill to travel and was not at the March inauguration. Alone at the White House, the new president felt hunted by men who wanted to be appointed to public offices. The White House was filled with job-seekers. They lounged about day after day, waiting to see Harrison. Hundreds of letters arrived each day from men who wanted the same thing—government jobs.

In late March, Harrison caught a cold while out doing his customary early-morning shopping. The cold worsened and soon turned into pneumonia. Doctors were summoned. They were not overly concerned at first, but Harrison knew how ill he really was. He told a nurse, "Ah, Fanny, I am ill, very ill, much more so than they think me."

The death of William Henry Harrison on April 4, 1841

On April 4, 1841, less than a week after he first caught cold, Harrison died at the White House. His last words showed that, as always, his first concern was his country: "Sir," he said to the doctor attending him, "I wish you to understand the principles of government. I wish them carried out. I ask nothing more."

Anna Harrison heard the news of her husband's death just as she was about to begin a trip to join him in Washington. Instead of joining him at the White House, Anna was in time to attend his memorial service on April 7. Then she brought him home to be buried at North Bend. Today, his tomb stands on a slight hill overlooking the Ohio River and the western lands that Harrison served so well and loved so long.

Chronology of American History

(Shaded area covers events in William Henry Harrison's lifetime.)

About A.D. 982 — Eric the Red, born in Norway, reaches Greenland in one of the first European voyages to North America.

About 985 — Eric the Red brings settlers from Iceland to Greenland.

About 1000 — Leif Ericson (Eric the Red's son) leads what is thought to be the first European expedition to mainland North America; Leif probably lands in Canada.

1492 — Christopher Columbus, seeking a sea route from Spain to the Far East, discovers the New World.

1497 — John Cabot reaches Canada in the first English voyage to North America.

1513 — Ponce de Léon explores Florida in search of the fabled Fountain of Youth.

1519-1521 — Hernando Cortés of Spain conquers Mexico.

1534 — French explorers led by Jacques Cartier enter the Gulf of St. Lawrence in Canada.

1540 — Spanish explorer Francisco Coronado begins exploring the American Southwest, seeking the riches of the mythical Seven Cities of Cibola.

1565 — St. Augustine, Florida, the first permanent European town in what is now the United States, is founded by the Spanish.

1607 — Jamestown, Virginia, is founded, the first permanent English town in the present-day U.S.

1608 — Frenchman Samuel de Champlain founds the village of Quebec, Canada.

1609 — Henry Hudson explores the eastern coast of present-day U.S. for the Netherlands; the Dutch then claim parts of New York, New Jersey, Delaware, and Connecticut and name the area New Netherland.

1619 — The English colonies' first shipment of black slaves arrives in Jamestown.

1620 — English Pilgrims found Massachusetts' first permanent town at Plymouth.

1621 — Massachusetts Pilgrims and Indians hold the famous first Thanksgiving feast in colonial America.

1623 — Colonization of New Hampshire is begun by the English.

1624 — Colonization of present-day New York State is begun by the Dutch at Fort Orange (Albany).

1625 — The Dutch start building New Amsterdam (now New York City).

1630 — The town of Boston, Massachusetts, is founded by the English Puritans.

1633 — Colonization of Connecticut is begun by the English.

1634 — Colonization of Maryland is begun by the English.

1636 — Harvard, the colonies' first college, is founded in Massachusetts. Rhode Island colonization begins when Englishman Roger Williams founds Providence.

1638 — Delaware colonization begins when Swedish people build Fort Christina at present-day Wilmington.

1640 — Stephen Daye of Cambridge, Massachusetts prints *The Bay Psalm Book*, the first English-language book published in what is now the U.S.

1643 — Swedish settlers begin colonizing Pennsylvania.

About 1650 — North Carolina is colonized by Virginia settlers.

1660 — New Jersey colonization is begun by the Dutch at present-day Jersey City.

1670 — South Carolina colonization is begun by the English near Charleston.

1673 — Jacques Marquette and Louis Jolliet explore the upper Mississippi River for France.

1682—Philadelphia, Pennsylvania, is settled. La Salle explores Mississippi River all the way to its mouth in Louisiana and claims the whole Mississippi Valley for France.

1693—College of William and Mary is founded in Williamsburg, Virginia.

1700—Colonial population is about 250,000.

1703—Benjamin Franklin is born in Boston.

1732—George Washington, first president of the U.S., is born in Westmoreland County, Virginia.

1733—James Oglethorpe founds Savannah, Georgia; Georgia is established as the thirteenth colony.

1735—John Adams, second president of the U.S., is born in Braintree, Massachusetts.

1737—William Byrd founds Richmond, Virginia.

1738—British troops are sent to Georgia over border dispute with Spain.

1739—Black insurrection takes place in South Carolina.

1740—English Parliament passes act allowing naturalization of immigrants to American colonies after seven-year residence.

1743—Thomas Jefferson, third president of the U.S., is born in Albemarle County, Virginia. Benjamin Franklin retires at age thirty-seven to devote himself to scientific inquiries and public service.

1744—King George's War begins; France joins war effort against England.

1745—During King George's War, France raids settlements in Maine and New York.

1747—Classes begin at Princeton College in New Jersey.

1748—The Treaty of Aix-la-Chapelle concludes King George's War.

1749—Parliament legally recognizes slavery in colonies and the inauguration of the plantation system in the South. George Washington becomes the surveyor for Culpepper County in Virginia.

1750—Thomas Walker passes through and names Cumberland Gap on his way toward Kentucky region. Colonial population is about 1,200,000.

1751—James Madison, fourth president of the U.S., is born in Port Conway, Virginia. English Parliament passes Currency Act, banning New England colonies from issuing paper money. George Washington travels to Barbados.

1752—Pennsylvania Hospital, the first general hospital in the colonies, is founded in Philadelphia. Benjamin Franklin uses a kite in a thunderstorm to demonstrate that lightning is a form of electricity.

1753—George Washington delivers command from Virginia Lieutenant Governor Dinwiddie that the French withdraw from the Ohio River Valley; French disregard the demand. Colonial population is about 1,328,000.

1754—French and Indian War begins (extends to Europe as the Seven Years' War). Washington surrenders at Fort Necessity.

1755—French and Indians ambush General Braddock. Washington becomes commander of Virginia troops.

1756—England declares war on France.

1758—James Monroe, fifth president of the U.S., is born in Westmoreland County, Virginia.

1759—Cherokee Indian war begins in southern colonies; hostilities extend to 1761. George Washington marries Martha Dandridge Custis.

1760—George III becomes king of England. Colonial population is about 1,600,000.

1762—England declares war on Spain.

1763—Treaty of Paris concludes the French and Indian War and the Seven Years' War. England gains Canada and most other French lands east of the Mississippi River.

1764—British pass the Sugar Act to gain tax money from the colonists. The issue of taxation without representation is first introduced in Boston. John Adams marries Abigail Smith.

1765—Stamp Act goes into effect in the colonies. Business virtually stops as almost all colonists refuse to use the stamps.

1766—British repeal the Stamp Act.

1767—John Quincy Adams, sixth president of the U.S. and son of second president John Adams, is born in Braintree, Massachusetts. Andrew Jackson, seventh president of the U.S., is born in Waxhaw settlement, South Carolina.

1769—Daniel Boone sights the Kentucky Territory.

1770—In the Boston Massacre, British soldiers kill five colonists and injure six. Townshend Acts are repealed, thus eliminating all duties on imports to the colonies except tea.

1771—Benjamin Franklin begins his autobiography, a work that he will never complete. The North Carolina assembly passes the "Bloody Act," which makes rioters guilty of treason.

1772—Samuel Adams rouses colonists to consider British threats to self-government. Thomas Jefferson marries Martha Wayles Skelton.

1773—English Parliament passes the Tea Act. Colonists dressed as Mohawk Indians board British tea ships and toss 342 casks of tea into the water in what becomes known as the Boston Tea Party. William Henry Harrison is born in Charles City County, Virginia.

1774—British close the port of Boston to punish the city for the Boston Tea Party. First Continental Congress convenes in Philadelphia.

1775—American Revolution begins with battles of Lexington and Concord, Massachusetts. Second Continental Congress opens in Philadelphia. George Washington becomes commander-in-chief of the Continental army.

1776—Declaration of Independence is adopted on July 4.

1777—Congress adopts the American flag with thirteen stars and thirteen stripes. John Adams is sent to France to negotiate peace treaty.

1778—France declares war against Great Britain and becomes U.S. ally.

1779—British surrender to Americans at Vincennes. Thomas Jefferson is elected governor of Virginia. James Madison is elected to the Continental Congress.

1780—Benedict Arnold, first American traitor, defects to the British.

1781—Articles of Confederation go into effect. Cornwallis surrenders to George Washington at Yorktown, ending the American Revolution.

1782—American commissioners, including John Adams, sign peace treaty with British in Paris. Thomas Jefferson's wife, Martha, dies. Martin Van Buren is born in Kinderhook, New York.

1784—Zachary Taylor is born near Barboursville, Virginia.

1785—Congress adopts the dollar as the unit of currency. John Adams is made minister to Great Britain. Thomas Jefferson is appointed minister to France.

1786—Shays' Rebellion begins in Massachusetts.

1787—Constitutional Convention assembles in Philadelphia, with George Washington presiding; U.S. Constitution is adopted. Delaware, New Jersey, and Pennsylvania become states.

1788—Virginia, South Carolina, New York, Connecticut, New Hampshire, Maryland, and Massachusetts become states. U.S. Constitution is ratified. New York City is declared U.S. capital.

1789—Presidential electors elect George Washington and John Adams as first president and vice-president. Thomas Jefferson is appointed secretary of state. North Carolina becomes a state. French Revolution begins.

1790—Supreme Court meets for the first time. Rhode Island becomes a state. First national census in the U.S. counts 3,929,214 persons. John Tyler is born in Charles City County, Virginia.

1791 — Vermont enters the Union. U.S. Bill of Rights, the first ten amendments to the Constitution, goes into effect. District of Columbia is established.

1792 — Thomas Paine publishes *The Rights of Man*. Kentucky becomes a state. Two political parties are formed in the U.S., Federalist and Republican. Washington is elected to a second term, with Adams as vice-president.

1793 — War between France and Britain begins; U.S. declares neutrality. Eli Whitney invents the cotton gin; cotton production and slave labor increase in the South.

1794 — Eleventh Amendment to the Constitution is passed, limiting federal courts' power. "Whiskey Rebellion" in Pennsylvania protests federal whiskey tax. James Madison marries Dolley Payne Todd.

1795 — George Washington signs the Jay Treaty with Great Britain. Treaty of San Lorenzo, between U.S. and Spain, settles Florida boundary and gives U.S. right to navigate the Mississippi. James Polk is born near Pineville, North Carolina.

1796 — Tennessee enters the Union. Washington gives his Farewell Address, refusing a third presidential term. John Adams is elected president and Thomas Jefferson vice-president.

1797 — Adams recommends defense measures against possible war with France. Napoleon Bonaparte and his army march against Austrians in Italy. U.S. population is about 4,900,000.

1798 — Washington is named commander-in-chief of the U.S. army. Department of the Navy is created. Alien and Sedition Acts are passed. Napoleon's troops invade Egypt and Switzerland.

1799 — George Washington dies at Mount Vernon. James Monroe is elected governor of Virginia. French Revolution ends. Napoleon becomes ruler of France.

1800 — Thomas Jefferson and Aaron Burr tie for president. U.S. capital is moved from Philadelphia to Washington, D.C. The White House is built as presidents' home. Spain returns Louisiana to France. Millard Fillmore is born in Locke, New York.

1801 — After thirty-six ballots, House of Representatives elects Thomas Jefferson president, making Burr vice-president. James Madison is named secretary of state.

1802 — Congress abolishes excise taxes. U.S. Military Academy is founded at West Point, New York.

1803 — Ohio enters the Union. Louisiana Purchase treaty is signed with France, greatly expanding U.S. territory.

1804 — Twelfth Amendment to the Constitution rules that president and vice-president be elected separately. Alexander Hamilton is killed by Vice-President Aaron Burr in a duel. Orleans Territory is established. Napoleon crowns himself emperor of France.

1805 — Thomas Jefferson begins his second term as president. Lewis and Clark expedition reaches the Pacific Ocean.

1806 — Coinage of silver dollars is stopped; resumes in 1836.

1807 — Aaron Burr is acquitted in treason trial. Embargo Act closes U.S. ports to trade.

1808 — James Madison is elected president. Congress outlaws importing slaves from Africa.

1810 — U.S. population is 7,240,000.

1811 — William Henry Harrison defeats Indians at Tippecanoe. Monroe is named secretary of state.

1812 — Louisiana becomes a state. U.S. declares war on Britain (War of 1812). James Madison is reelected president. Napoleon invades Russia.

1813 — British forces take Fort Niagara and Buffalo, New York.

1814 — Francis Scott Key writes "The Star-Spangled Banner." British troops burn much of Washington, D.C., including the White House. Treaty of Ghent ends War of 1812. James Monroe becomes secretary of war.

1815 — Napoleon meets his final defeat at Battle of Waterloo.

1816 — James Monroe is elected president. Indiana becomes a state.

1817 — Mississippi becomes a state. Construction on Erie Canal begins.

1818—Illinois enters the Union. The present thirteen-stripe flag is adopted. Border between U.S. and Canada is agreed upon.

1819—Alabama becomes a state. U.S. purchases Florida from Spain. Thomas Jefferson establishes the University of Virginia.

1820—James Monroe is reelected. In the Missouri Compromise, Maine enters the Union as a free (non-slave) state.

1821—Missouri enters the Union as a slave state. Santa Fe Trail opens the American Southwest. Mexico declares independence from Spain. Napoleon Bonaparte dies.

1822—U.S. recognizes Mexico and Colombia. Liberia in Africa is founded as a home for freed slaves.

1823—Monroe Doctrine closes North and South America to European colonizing or invasion.

1824—House of Representatives elects John Quincy Adams president when none of the four candidates wins a majority in national election. Mexico becomes a republic.

1825—Erie Canal is opened. U.S. population is 11,300,000.

1826—Thomas Jefferson and John Adams both die on July 4, the fiftieth anniversary of the Declaration of Independence.

1828—Andrew Jackson is elected president. Tariff of Abominations is passed, cutting imports.

1829—James Madison attends Virginia's constitutional convention. Slavery is abolished in Mexico.

1830—Indian Removal Act to resettle Indians west of the Mississippi is approved.

1831—James Monroe dies in New York City. James A. Garfield is born in Orange, Ohio. Cyrus McCormick develops his reaper.

1832—Andrew Jackson, nominated by the new Democratic Party, is reelected president.

1833—Britain abolishes slavery in its colonies.

1835—Federal government becomes debt-free for the first time.

1836—Martin Van Buren becomes president. Texas wins independence from Mexico. Arkansas joins the Union. James Madison dies at Montpelier, Virginia.

1837—Michigan enters the Union. U.S. population is 15,900,000.

1840—William Henry Harrison is elected president.

1841—President Harrison dies in Washington, D.C., one month after inauguration. Vice-President John Tyler succeeds him.

1844—James Knox Polk is elected president. Samuel Morse sends first telegraphic message.

1845—Texas and Florida become states. Potato famine in Ireland causes massive emigration from Ireland to U.S. Andrew Jackson dies near Nashville, Tennessee.

1846—Iowa enters the Union. War with Mexico begins.

1847—U.S. captures Mexico City.

1848—Zachary Taylor becomes president. Treaty of Guadalupe Hidalgo ends Mexico-U.S. war. Wisconsin becomes a state.

1849—James Polk dies in Nashville, Tennessee.

1850—President Taylor dies in Washington, D.C.; Vice-President Millard Fillmore succeeds him. California enters the Union, breaking tie between slave and free states.

1852—Franklin Pierce is elected president.

1853—Gadsden Purchase transfers Mexican territory to U.S.

1854—"War for Bleeding Kansas" is fought between slave and free states.

1855—Czar Nicholas I of Russia dies, succeeded by Alexander II.

1856—James Buchanan is elected president. In Massacre of Potawatomi Creek, Kansas-slavers are murdered by free-staters.

1858 — Minnesota enters the Union. Theodore Roosevelt is born in New York City.

1859 — Oregon becomes a state.

1860 — Abraham Lincoln is elected president; South Carolina secedes from the Union in protest.

1861 — Arkansas, Tennessee, North Carolina, and Virginia secede. Kansas enters the Union as a free state. Civil War begins.

1862 — Union forces capture Fort Henry, Roanoke Island, Fort Donelson, Jacksonville, and New Orleans; Union armies are defeated at the battles of Bull Run and Fredericksburg. Martin Van Buren dies in Kinderhook, New York. John Tyler dies near Charles City, Virginia.

1863 — Lincoln issues Emancipation Proclamation: all slaves held in rebelling territories are declared free. West Virginia becomes a state.

1864 — Abraham Lincoln is reelected. Nevada becomes a state.

1865 — Lincoln is assassinated, succeeded by Andrew Johnson. U.S. Civil War ends on May 26. Thirteenth Amendment abolishes slavery.

1867 — Nebraska becomes a state. U.S. buys Alaska from Russia for $7,200,000. Reconstruction Acts are passed.

1868 — President Johnson is impeached for violating Tenure of Office Act, but is acquitted by Senate. Ulysses S. Grant is elected president. Fourteenth Amendment prohibits voting discrimination.

1870 — Fifteenth Amendment gives blacks the right to vote.

1872 — Grant is reelected over Horace Greeley. General Amnesty Act pardons ex-Confederates.

1874 — Millard Fillmore dies in Buffalo, New York. Herbert Hoover is born in West Branch, Iowa.

1876 — Colorado enters the Union. "Custer's last stand": he and his men are massacred by Sioux Indians at Little Big Horn, Montana.

1877 — Rutherford B. Hayes is elected president as all disputed votes are awarded to him.

1880 — James A. Garfield is elected president.

1881 — President Garfield is assassinated and dies in Elberon, New Jersey. Vice-President Chester A. Arthur succeeds him.

1882 — U.S. bans Chinese immigration. Franklin D. Roosevelt is born in Hyde Park, New York.

1884 — Grover Cleveland is elected president.

1886 — Statue of Liberty is dedicated.

1888 — Benjamin Harrison is elected president.

1889 — North Dakota, South Dakota, Washington, and Montana become states.

1890 — Dwight D. Eisenhower is born in Denison, Texas. Idaho and Wyoming become states.

1892 — Grover Cleveland is elected president.

1896 — William McKinley is elected president. Utah becomes a state.

1898 — U.S. declares war on Spain over Cuba.

1900 — McKinley is reelected. Boxer Rebellion against foreigners in China begins.

1901 — McKinley is assassinated by anarchist; he is succeeded by Theodore Roosevelt.

1902 — U.S. acquires perpetual control over Panama Canal.

1903 — Alaskan frontier is settled.

1904 — Russian-Japanese War breaks out. Theodore Roosevelt wins presidential election.

1905 — Treaty of Portsmouth signed, ending Russian-Japanese War.

1906 — U.S. troops occupy Cuba.

1907 — President Roosevelt bars all Japanese immigration. Oklahoma enters the Union.

1908 — William Howard Taft becomes president. Lyndon B. Johnson is born near Stonewall, Texas.

1909—NAACP is founded under W.E.B. DuBois

1910—China abolishes slavery.

1911—Chinese Revolution begins.

1912—Woodrow Wilson is elected president. Arizona and New Mexico become states.

1913—Federal income tax is introduced in U.S. through the Sixteenth Amendment. Richard Nixon is born in Yorba Linda, California.

1914—World War I begins.

1915—British liner *Lusitania* is sunk by German submarine.

1916—Wilson is reelected president.

1917—U.S. breaks diplomatic relations with Germany. Czar Nicholas of Russia abdicates as revolution begins. U.S. declares war on Austria-Hungary. John F. Kennedy is born in Brookline, Massachusetts.

1918—Wilson proclaims "Fourteen Points" as war aims. On November 11, armistice is signed between Allies and Germany.

1919—Eighteenth Amendment prohibits sale and manufacture of intoxicating liquors. Wilson presides over first League of Nations; wins Nobel Peace Prize. Theodore Roosevelt dies in Oyster Bay, New York.

1920—Nineteenth Amendment (women's suffrage) is passed. Warren Harding is elected president.

1921—Adolf Hitler's stormtroopers begin to terrorize political opponents.

1922—Irish Free State is established. Soviet states form USSR. Benito Mussolini forms Fascist government in Italy.

1923—President Harding dies; he is succeeded by Vice-President Calvin Coolidge.

1924—Coolidge is elected president.

1925—Hitler reorganizes Nazi Party and publishes first volume of *Mein Kampf.*

1926—Fascist youth organizations founded in Germany and Italy. Republic of Lebanon proclaimed.

1927—Stalin becomes Soviet dictator. Economic conference in Geneva attended by fifty-two nations.

1928—Herbert Hoover is elected president. U.S. and many other nations sign Kellogg-Briand pacts to outlaw war.

1929—Stock prices in New York crash on "Black Thursday"; the Great Depression begins.

1930—Bank of U.S. and its many branches close (most significant bank failure of the year).

1931—Emigration from U.S. exceeds immigration for first time as Depression deepens.

1932—Franklin D. Roosevelt wins presidential election in a Democratic landslide.

1933—First concentration camps are erected in Germany. U.S. recognizes USSR and resumes trade. Twenty-First Amendment repeals prohibition.

1934—Severe dust storms hit Plains states. President Roosevelt passes U.S. Social Security Act.

1936—Roosevelt is reelected. Spanish Civil War begins. Hitler and Mussolini form Rome-Berlin Axis.

1937—Roosevelt signs Neutrality Act.

1938—Roosevelt sends appeal to Hitler and Mussolini to settle European problems amicably.

1939—Germany takes over Czechoslovakia and invades Poland, starting World War II.

1940—Roosevelt is reelected for a third term.

1941—Japan bombs Pearl Harbor. U.S. declares war on Japan. Germany and Italy declare war on U.S.; U.S. then declares war on them.

1942—Allies agree not to make separate peace treaties with the enemies. U.S. government transfers more than 100,000 Nisei (Japanese-Americans) from west coast to inland concentration camps.

1943 — Allied bombings of Germany begin.

1944 — Roosevelt is reelected for a fourth term. Allied forces invade Normandy on D-Day.

1945 — President Franklin D. Roosevelt dies in Warm Springs, Georgia; Vice-President Harry S. Truman succeeds him. Mussolini is killed; Hitler commits suicide. Germany surrenders. U.S. drops atomic bomb on Hiroshima; Japan surrenders: end of World War II.

1946 — U.N. General Assembly holds its first session in London. Peace conference of twenty-one nations is held in Paris.

1947 — Peace treaties are signed in Paris. "Cold War" is in full swing.

1948 — U.S. passes Marshall Plan Act, providing $17 billion in aid for Europe. U.S. recognizes new nation of Israel. India and Pakistan become free of British rule. Truman is elected president.

1949 — Republic of Eire is proclaimed in Dublin. Russia blocks land route access from Western Germany to Berlin; airlift begins. U.S., France, and Britain agree to merge their zones of occupation in West Germany. Apartheid program begins in South Africa.

1950 — Riots in Johannesburg, South Africa, against apartheid. North Korea invades South Korea. U.N. forces land in South Korea and recapture Seoul.

1951 — Twenty-Second Amendment limits president to two terms.

1952 — Dwight D. Eisenhower resigns as supreme commander in Europe and is elected president.

1953 — Stalin dies; struggle for power in Russia follows. Rosenbergs are executed for espionage.

1954 — U.S. and Japan sign mutual defense agreement.

1955 — Blacks in Montgomery, Alabama, boycott segregated bus lines.

1956 — Eisenhower is reelected president. Soviet troops march into Hungary.

1957 — U.S. agrees to withdraw ground forces from Japan. Russia launches first satellite, *Sputnik.*

1958 — European Common Market comes into being. Alaska becomes the forty-ninth state. Fidel Castro begins war against Batista government in Cuba.

1959 — Hawaii becomes fiftieth state. Castro becomes premier of Cuba. De Gaulle is proclaimed president of the Fifth Republic of France.

1960 — Historic debates between Senator John F. Kennedy and Vice-President Richard Nixon are televised. Kennedy is elected president. Brezhnev becomes president of USSR.

1961 — Berlin Wall is constructed. Kennedy and Khrushchev confer in Vienna. In Bay of Pigs incident, Cubans trained by CIA attempt to overthrow Castro.

1962 — U.S. military council is established in South Vietnam.

1963 — Riots and beatings by police and whites mark civil rights demonstrations in Birmingham, Alabama; 30,000 troops are called out, Martin Luther King, Jr., is arrested. Freedom marchers descend on Washington, D.C., to demonstrate. President Kennedy is assassinated in Dallas, Texas; Vice-President Lyndon B. Johnson is sworn in as president.

1964 — U.S. aircraft bomb North Vietnam. Johnson is elected president. Herbert Hoover dies in New York City.

1965 — U.S. combat troops arrive in South Vietnam.

1966 — Thousands protest U.S. policy in Vietnam. National Guard quells race riots in Chicago.

1967 — Six-Day War between Israel and Arab nations.

1968 — Martin Luther King, Jr., is assassinated in Memphis, Tennessee. Senator Robert Kennedy is assassinated in Los Angeles. Riots and police brutality take place at Democratic National Convention in Chicago. Richard Nixon is elected president. Czechoslovakia is invaded by Soviet troops.

1969 — Dwight D. Eisenhower dies in Washington, D.C. Hundreds of thousands of people in several U.S. cities demonstrate against Vietnam War.

1970—Four Vietnam War protesters are killed by National Guardsmen at Kent State University in Ohio.

1971—Twenty-Sixth Amendment allows eighteen-year-olds to vote.

1972—Nixon visits Communist China; is reelected president in near-record landslide. Watergate affair begins when five men are arrested in the Watergate hotel complex in Washington, D.C. Nixon announces resignations of aides Haldeman, Ehrlichman, and Dean and Attorney General Kleindienst as a result of Watergate-related charges. Harry S. Truman dies in Kansas City, Missouri.

1973—Vice-President Spiro Agnew resigns; Gerald Ford is named vice-president. Vietnam peace treaty is formally approved after nineteen months of negotiations. Lyndon B. Johnson dies in San Antonio, Texas.

1974—As a result of Watergate cover-up, impeachment is considered; Nixon resigns and Ford becomes president. Ford pardons Nixon and grants limited amnesty to Vietnam War draft evaders and military deserters.

1975—U.S. civilians are evacuated from Saigon, South Vietnam, as Communist forces complete takeover of South Vietnam.

1976—U.S. celebrates its Bicentennial. James Earl Carter becomes president.

1977—Carter pardons most Vietnam draft evaders, numbering some 10,000.

1980—Ronald Reagan is elected president.

1981—President Reagan is shot in the chest in assassination attempt. Sandra Day O'Connor is appointed first woman justice of the Supreme Court.

1983—U.S. troops invade island of Grenada.

1984—Reagan is reelected president. Democratic candidate Walter Mondale's running mate, Geraldine Ferraro, is the first woman selected for vice-president by a major U.S. political party.

1985—Soviet Communist Party secretary Konstantin Chernenko dies; Mikhail Gorbachev succeeds him. U.S. and Soviet officials discuss arms control in Geneva. Reagan and Gorbachev hold summit conference in Geneva. Racial tensions accelerate in South Africa.

1986—Space shuttle *Challenger* explodes shortly after takeoff; crew of seven dies. U.S. bombs bases in Libya. Corazon Aquino defeats Ferdinand Marcos in Philippine presidential election.

1987—Iraqi missile rips the U.S. frigate *Stark* in the Persian Gulf, killing thirty-seven American sailors. Congress holds hearings to investigate sale of U.S. arms to Iran to finance Nicaraguan *contra* movement.

1988—George Bush is elected president. President Reagan and Soviet leader Gorbachev sign INF treaty, eliminating intermediate nuclear forces. Severe drought sweeps the United States.

Index

Page numbers in boldface type indicate illustrations.

About the Author

Christine Fitz-Gerald has a B.A. in English Literature from Ohio University and a Masters in Management from Northwestern University. She has been employed by the Quaker Oats Company and by General Mills. Most recently, she was a strategic planner for a division of Honeywell, Inc. in Minneapolis. She now resides in Chicago with her husband and three young children. Her Childrens Press titles include *I Can Be a Reporter* and *Encyclopedia of Presidents: James Monroe*.